# River of Bones

# River of Bones

Poems

## Holly Guran

Iris Press
Oak Ridge, Tennessee

Cover and Section Photographs by Philip L. McAlary

Book Design by Robert B. Cumming, Jr.

Library of Congress Cataloging-in-Publication Data

Guran, Holly.
  [Poems. Selections]
  River of bones : poems / Holly Guran.
      pages cm
    ISBN 978-1-60454-228-8 (pbk. : alk. paper)
    I. Title.
    PS3607.U5486.A6 2014
    811'.6—dc23
                                    2014041965

## ACKNOWLEDGMENTS

*The Aurorean*: "At the River's Frozen Bank"
*Bellowing Ark*: "Home," "Summer Marshfield"
*Big Muddy*: "Green Heron," "Marsh"
*The Blotter Magazine*: "Sam's Advice"
*Borderlands*: "Turn-Out"
*Cavan Kerry Press, The Breath of Parted Lips* anthology: "River Tracks"
*Em-Dash*: "Weird"
*Explorations*: "Cranberry Harvest"
*Gihon River Review*: "Wild River"
*Hawai'i Pacific Review*: "Jazz Piano"
*Moon Magazine*: "It Says," "The Committee Responds," "Regulations"
*Noctiluca Magazine*: "Forest Trail"
*Poetry East*: "Applause"
*Poet Lore*: "Resilient," "Two-Cent Bridge"
*Postcard Poems and Prose*: "Fight for the Ten Hour Day"
*San Pedro River Review*: "Shock Treatment"
*Soundings*: "Sunset at Pier 60"
*U.S. 1 Worksheets*: "Marion Cemetery"
*Westchester Review*: "Ark"
*Worcester Review*: "I Learned from the Webs of Cloth"
*Zymbol*, forthcoming: "To Cleanse"

Poets Corner Press *River Tracks* chapbook: "Cranberry Harvest," "Grape Jelly," "On Peter's Hill," "Phragmites"

Noctiluca Press *Mothers' Trails* chapbook: "This Life," "Home," "Window"

Boston City Hall following Boston Marathon Bombing: "Hot Wind" and "To Cleanse" posted

*Explorations* poetry contest: "Cranberry Harvest," 2nd place

I am deeply grateful to the many individuals whose intelligent responses helped the poems and the manuscript grow: the astute and generous Joiner Institute instructors Martha Collins and Bruce Weigl; long-term mentor and poetry colleague, Judy Katz-Levine; Carolyn Gregory who introduced me to her talented Saturday morning crew of Jamaica Pond Poets, Dorothy Derifield, Audrey Henderson, Susanna Kittredge, Alice Kociemba, Dorian Kotsiopoulos, Jim Lafond-Lewis, Jennifer Markell, Sybille Rex, Sandra Storey, and Gary Whited.

Thank you Bob and Beto Cumming for believing in my work.

Thank you husband Phil for your patience and listening, for the inspiring photographs that grace the book's cover and sections.

For Phil

# CONTENTS

III. ARK

EPILOGUE

*Time flies over us, but leaves its shadow behind.*

—Nathaniel Hawthorne

# PROLOGUE

## Phragmites

Golden the phragmites as light
splashes them, a black line where
water joins. Mirror, dark mirror,
effervescing flotsam on top, below
a sliding layer, submerged leaves, decay,
sticks as far from here
the tide sucks in the river.

Our canoe barely leaks
and the hawks dip in pairs
at first haphazard
then in tandem hungry
poised for the dive.
A lone muskrat's shining fur,
our dark underwater path

and ahead the golden
phragmites and all around they
barely speak in silent tongues
a wall between water
and shore they grow uncontrollably
hold the marsh mysteries
in papery stalks and tassels.

They swallow the river at its bend
leave us with a dark channel ahead
whose course is hidden, dense—
an invitation.

# I

## UNSTEADY CRADLE

## UNSTEADY CRADLE ROCKING

babies long grown up and gone
great-grandfather writes
in 1927 to his son
> *How full the world, narcissus in full bloom.*
> *I'm watching plans for the Colorado River.*
> *Streets being paved, sidewalks laid.*
> *We turn away applicants.*

then 1930...
the change profound bore down on new roads
crushed plans
> *Can't sell and hard to rent.*
> *Many men out of work.*
> *Hope to see you in California on no distant day.*
> *Perhaps you would settle here.*

wishing for a son to ease the fear
drive the long miles
inject hope into the troubles
> *Now I'm short on funds to meet the taxes.*
> *Can you help me out?*
> *I made some mistakes in investments,*
> *thank you for your check.*

loyal son helped with money
never made the trip too far
his own life, his own fortune's slings
> *Times have been so dull*
> *our income barely enough*
> *to keep us from hand to mouth.*
> *I long to see your faces and grasp your hands.*

downed by depression's arrow
sons and daughters too far
he made do, ate what the garden grew
  *It tires me to write.*
  *Hard to get everything to work.*
  *The light, the glare on my glasses don't jibe.*
  *If you can see your way, point your car toward us.*

## From California

I wish to stroll your Hudson farm's hills and hollows,
so many acres stretch between our separate coasts.
Up in the barn behind the house, can you see the swallows?
I wish to walk over familiar hills and hollows.
Moving here I didn't expect depression would follow,
didn't know your face would become faint as a ghost.
I wish to walk over those familiar hills and hollows,
so much land grows between our separate coasts.

## CRANBERRY HARVEST

A man sitting high on the harvester steers
through the bog in a circle.
Cranberries swell a palette at the edge.
The man wears black rubber pants.

How cold it must get
sitting just above the water
as the rotating blades free the berries
to bob and cluster.

Farming—it looks easy!  Plants submerged
under water, maple and oak beginning to flame
in the distance, moist grass thick underfoot.

My uncle harvested apples
large and red onto the flatbed truck,
crates piled and ready for the barn.

You don't see how hard it is
relying on weather, God's invisible hand
or nature's. What if it freezes
when it's not supposed to,

or you can't spray and you can't stop
what's eating your cranberries or your apples,
and everything you own
is tied up in the harvest?

Brilliant color. Dark water. Cold legs. Long days.
The circle grows smaller,
cranberries accumulate. My uncle

rode out on the farm,
locked himself in his car, not
coming home, not coming home to the crispness
of apples piled in crates, the new packing house,
his family, debt.

He drifted out across the field,
and at last I catch a glimpse of him
in the cranberries and the dark water
that relinquishes them,

and the man intent on the water
driving his rig around the perimeter
in a narrowing spiral,
driving until the surface recedes,
until the cranberries
and jagged light fill in.

## OUTING

On our way to the Rockettes and a movie
because that's what people like us did,
out the train's dusty window,
we saw the Hudson, gray and moving,
on the other side the rocky Palisades,
then *the city* of high-rise towers.

At 125<sup>th</sup> Street the scenery changed.
I was young seeing what I'd never seen:
the forlorn face of endless tenements
and rickety fire escapes,
streets a confetti of flying paper,

a glimpse of black folks
walking or crossing,
block after block,
a film's arrested frames.
One woman staring leaned on her sill
to avoid the heat inside,

and I didn't understand why
any of this and kept asking
and no one said.
Then suddenly we were inside the tunnel
nearing Grand Central,
and Harlem disappeared.

## Jazz Piano

*for Charles Gayle*

A shadow stretches
high against the painted
building. Notes gallop
down into your fingers
becoming sounds.
Memory's crushing footsteps
strike on ahead, and
those who came before
deliver their echoes.
Suddenly two girls
skip hand in hand
along the sidewalk.
You cross the street
under the elevated subway
zooming overhead.
Cabs dart and weave.
The shadow reaches up
the painted building
where fire escapes
cascade down.
You travel them
one by one
in a zigzag pattern—
endless flights of fire escapes
though soon you'll rise
on the arpeggiated platforms
lifted by a host of cranes,
one level then the next
and you're calling
or maybe it's a shout—

*I offer you a gateway*
*outside time and space*
*my shadow opens*
*enter here*

# Marsh

Inky silt slid from our blonde oars,
grabbed and held them
in the river's shallows—
a slime, a staining mix,

this ancient mud of living
creatures—primordial ooze
I could rub into my skin
and into yours.

We could bathe ourselves
and emerge darkened,
of different hues, to swim
just below the surface

growing more amphibious,
needing less air
until at last without question
we would belong here.

## Distant Summers

*the noontime of devoted families...*
*hour of silence*

Oh that joy of sun on water,
the feel of lake-soaked skin,
the piney smell permeating every tread
and inside each cabin, new wood.

Our two weeks at the lake
in Papago family cabin
with a native American name—
we say Indian—as close as we come.

> Ancestor Samuel trades *2.2 bushels*
> *of corn for 7 acres* in 1641,
> a piece of Chief Ponus's broad earth.

> Samuel's clan fences their fields
> *a certain number of rodd*
> *for every acre he hath then.*

In the circle of cabins, a group of friends.
Cocktails before dinner and after
we are fed. Our parents drink
into night, noisily play bridge.

Noon is quiet. We rest for an hour.
It passes, we rush to the beach, dive in,
hear the splash of displaced water
rising off the lake. The silence ends.

> Chief Ponus angers. His land's
> coralled, wooden structures glued
> to ground, fine roots of spirit wrenched.
> Cries pierce the silence several hours past noon.

## DADDY'S GIRL

I'm in junior high. We work side by side
in the basement. You fix
what's broken in the house,
sometimes complain about mother.
I feel privileged, uneasy.

I type school papers,
ask questions, waiting for the slow
delivery of your response.
Remember the paper about deep sea divers—
among the first to journey down,

lowered by stages into heavier waters?
Coming up they'd get the bends.
Nitrogen bubbles formed in their blood.
I marvel at anyone
willing to travel into darkness

and return. Overhead we hear footsteps,
the phone, noises from the kitchen
and the open windows.
I long for the upstairs world.

## TORNADO

you stop eating    then see
      the mile-long row of houses    leveled
your doctor's house    standing
      roof gone    windows shattered

    *Mother's letter tells of your silence*
    *through dinners, no going out.*
    *She's left alone, her walls close in.*

you    amazed    watch your doctor rise
      calm to greet you    as he always has
although the man    across his street
      walks into the storm    and is gone

    *She writes: the doctor advises treatment,*
    *electric shock, but she won't sign,*
    *thinks your body won't survive, down to 110.*

you stay indoors    away from
      the broken string of houses    eventually
start to eat    gain weight
      enough to hold you down

## SHOCK TREATMENT

The first spring I live away,
coming home I find you
wandering. You stand and talk,
even smile, mostly stare off
somewhere and take pictures,
pointing the camera at me

as you've always done, this time
empty—broken father,
a fractured vertebra, chalky
marks on either side of your forehead
where the shock went in.

Remember our guinea pig
whose cage was near your workbench?
That time the neighbor's dog
got in, I was late
coming home from school.

Spotty held the broken guinea pig
between his teeth then
slinked away for a mad chase
after the next car.
We all expected he'd get hit,
but he died quietly in his sleep.

That summer as the maple leaves
turned plainer green, you
seemed to die and didn't, smiling
like an actor in a silent film, sitting
in the special chair made of cherry,
shaped so you wouldn't feel the pain.

## SAILOR DREAM

Waving and smiling you come back.
You can see the shore now.

Soon you may even enter the water
to wade and swim again.

Welcome, welcome back in your boat
with the string of pointed flags aflutter.

The storm has lifted for you
to see the fishes, the others boats, me.

Sun on your face sheds rainbow colors,
even the deep color

of your leaving belongs to this
arrival and shows me how

to hold your hand and tells me—
when your boat sails

over the edge…

# Under the Trees

You are older this year.
They have made
a diagnosis,
then promises:
radiation, remission.

And now time for us
to sit beside the river,
each in an unfolded
lawn chair, talking
under the trees,

sachets of time,
to keep in the drawer
later, sweetening what I wear,
softening the hard edges—
my life, this bureau.

Is it wrong
to want you near?
I have always feared your closeness.
Outside the trees,
heavy with white blossoms,
lower themselves into the river.

# GRAPE JELLY

My grown son watched the Concord grapes
ripen in his city yard, and when he'd picked them,
and their sweetness swirled over the boiling pot,
he insisted we should imitate my mother

who'd taken grapes last fall
and crushed them, boiled the juice.
It had dripped all night through a bag
of cheesecloth in my kitchen, hung by a pole
resting on two chairs.

She had imitated my father—
her contraption had his style in it.
A man whose body worried him,
he'd retreat to fix what came apart.

She had done it his way,
and when we returned from burying her ashes,
we all remembered her complaint:
he would tell her how to do things, like drying dishes,

just so, and we all laughed that family laugh
that's loud and forgetful,
full of the remembering
no one really wants

that comes down the dark vine's juices,
purple dripping all night,
long nights
in death's grip.

Then she grew lighter.
We were bathing her—
that rattle, a rasping sound, metal
scraping dry wood.

My son would create his own device for dripping juices,
a deep bucket scrubbed clean
of any trace of spackle,
a circle of cheesecloth suspended over the rim.

At first I doubted,
but then I watched
the cheesecloth holding
its weight of little skins
as the white bucket filled with purple liquid.

## Resilient

A kind of cloth envelope
meant to hold hankies or trinkets
a girl might cherish, its cover
a peach-colored maybe-satin
but rougher, its insides
a darker flesh of velvet
with a stitched pattern of  diamonds.

The outside of this pouch—
yes, I think kangaroo—stained by time,
more than sixty years since it passed
to my hands from the neighbors
who moved in at night,
shocked my parents and the other white folks
on our block, two doors down
in the large house with a front porch.

Very young I made my visits
eating orange slices where we sat
on the porch and rocked the glider.
Either side of me the dark-skinned women
gathered laughter in their stitches.
Hush.    Listen.    There's a hum,
a murmur.    Voices in this velvet
my hand touches.

# A Hot Wind

I used to take a breath and
another bedtime would arrive,
me flossing my teeth.

Now the weeks slip, even the fish
Fridays of a generation have left
nearly as soon as they arrived.

My entire city's on lockdown
and time doesn't notice
doesn't even pause

though to us it seems caught
in a loop of sparse
news that spins and winds.

Don't open the door unless
a uniformed officer is standing
ready to search from basement to attic.

Okay fine. How long will this order
hold? Is this now or another loop of time
in league with the hot wind that blows?

# WINDOW

As darkness was tucking in the railroad bed
and all that lay ahead, the room
began to write its story—
shelves of paperbacks, bright toys,
me holding the baby—all reflected.

Beyond the glass, shadows danced
near the foot of the pine.
The train's silver streak wailed past
carrying people home.

The baby slept in her perfect skin,
tiny hands open. I wished
my daughter this age again,
envied them the inevitable moment
just ahead when the shadow

would become this daughter—grown
woman home from work—red coat,
briefcase, beaming face, then,
baby and mother reuniting
in their ecstatic embrace.

Held by the scent
of the baby's breathing,
I listened for the rumbling signal—
my daughter coming home.

# THIS LIFE

This one I give you
the only one I've ever known.
Although the remains
of other lives comfort.

They too bore down in childbirth,
felt the baby's lips on the nipple,
the early thrill of sex and later
its long bed of pleasure.

They too looked on a changing world.
From torn land, buildings rose or fell.
The skies rumbled.
New vehicles sped faster.

Their teeth ached,
the pine-covered hill in the distance
began to blur, the sounds of conversation,
children's questions, grew fainter.

I live here in the village
where they once walked
before they, too,
had to surrender.

# II

## MILL LIFE

*I worked in the cotton mill all of my life,*
*Ain't got nothing but a barlow knife,*
*And it's hard times, cotton mill girls,*
*Hard times everywhere.*

## ARCHEOLOGY

A hundred forty years
      this house was here

time enough to collect
      what they dropped

or left outside and forgot

before the leaves toppled
      and snow    followed

hiding playthings    chinks of glass
      along with a host

of skeletons in pet graves    clinkers
      from the days of coal.

We turn the soil and this earth
      offers up the random

trinket or toy    cherished bits    not ours
      they belong to the place.

Even so we bring them in
      rinse them off    wonder

about the young ones
      sent out to play

and the others
      who paced these rooms

rainy days    when the death bed held
      and despair rang

like church bells in the square.
       There must have been births

too    water boiling    in the big kitchen
       a midwife    gathering up her tools

and men repairing    the broken parts
       waiting to hear the cry.

What  we resurrect    carries back
       so little of them.

## LOSING FATHER

after *A New England Girlhood*
by Lucy Larcom (1824-1893)

My first decided taste: a love
of hymns. Memorizing them
at four, as natural as breathing.

"Ye stars are but the shining dust
of my divine abode."
The hymns lent me wings.

Father believed the millennium was near.
His last writing in the sick room
computed the date. Once

as he stood praying I was struck
by his pale face, his deep
gaze reflected in the mirror,

and later lifted to a footstool
beside his coffin,
I saw the same look.

Now his words that guided us
are gone. Mother keeps wearing
her lace cap, the one

father loved. She's rosy-cheeked,
but her face shifts easily
to shadow. Mournful strains

sound in the meeting-house. Outside
the bobolinks, the buttercups,
but inside we hear

this barren land. It seems
our duty to be sorrowful.
To be good, must we be miserable?

I love earth better than heaven,
the air full of hymns,
the sea's deeper songs

and sister Emilie,
our Scherherazade of story-
tellers. We listen as twilight

becomes moonlight. She toughens
herself sleeping on a hard
sea-chest. Before dawn,

runs white-robed barefoot
to the burying ground.
I dream of father as if

he were here. Mother,
left with eight of us,
prepares dinner downcast.

She misses a full larder.
I sing her my hymns.

## I Learned from the Webs of Cloth

*after A New England Girlhood*

I defied the machinery to make me its slave
to lift above annoyances          we have no control
I know that I was glad to be alive
separate   yet we entirely belong to the Whole

to lift above annoyances          we have no control
the girls were bright-looking          everything kept shining
separate          yet we entirely belong to the Whole
backwards and forwards          among the frames stooping

the girls were bright-looking          everything kept shining
accustomed to the noise          it became a silence
backwards and forwards          among the frames stooping
oh that I had wings for thoughts          and patience

accustomed to the noise          it became a silence
alone a web of cloth is a useless filament
oh that I had wings for thoughts          and patience
being part of a whole is all so different

alone a web of cloth is a useless filament
I know that I was glad to be alive
human beings are not mere mass
I made the machine my helper          I am not its slave

## BAKING THE MILL CAKE

Take one power loom model not permitted out of England.
Add a man with sharp memory, stealth.

Mix in new wealth that abhors a vacuum.
Roll out the five-story mills of brick.

Season with eager "girls"

> whose parents have died
> whose brothers want to study
> who are allowed to teach only in summer
> who must leave the farm.

Fold in the ideal: doing good and doing well.
Stir all in the bowl of rapid rivers tumbling over falls.

Turn on the oven of overseers, managers.
Turn on the looms. Add bales of cotton from the south.
Bake the rough white fabric for slaves to wear.
Bake the fine fabric to clothe everyone else.

## New at the Boott Cotton Mill, 1836

Two in a bed, four in a room,
my trunk pushed under.

Wherever there's a vacancy or spare corner
there I must locate with a stranger.

I mind this constant hurry,
wake in the dark to the 4:30 bell

then downstairs where the table's set
with patterned dishes,

and eat as quickly as I can
while they tease me about my accent—

call me rustic—
they from the farms as I am.

> *clig clag  clig clag  clig clag  clig clag*
> *a rhythm in 4/4 time*

> *from outside almost musical, inside*
> *the looms are great horses pounding*

I'm new, and so spare hand to one
who knows the weaving—

strong warp to the soft weft
interlacing into fabric, the colors

will show, but oh, my ears ring—I pray to hear
this throbbing as music, try to hold hymns

from Sunday—mine and the others' voices
invisible in the din. We talk in gestures.

From floor to ceiling heat climbs our skin,
steam spray makes us sweat.

The precious threads mustn't dry
and break—they've told me that.

If I make a mistake, the piece
will have to be discarded

and that means less. My parents need
whatever I can send.

At noon the bells toll us to the house
to rush through dinner

then back to toil in the lamp's dim light
until supper and a weary sit in the parlor.

We scramble for water to wash ourselves
before lights out. The bell tolls, at ten we fall into bed.

# From Farm and Barn to Lowell Mill

a scooter bonnet, a city way of speaking
> *a shawl pinned under the chin*
> *rustic twang*

feet that ache and swell
> *bare feet stepping through fields of corn*
> *Passampscot swamp lit by fireflies*

city lights twinkling in the gloom
girls nearby everywhere
> *on the farm young siblings waiting to be fed*

crimples, ruffs, puffs and farthingales
> *a plain wool dress*
> *a face brown from sun*

cheeks a carmine tint of rouge
larger right hand that stops and starts the loom
> *a balanced set of hands for milking*
> *for kneading bread*

wages to spend or send home or save
> *long hours laboring without pay*

meat twice a day
> *Sunday chicken (usually)*

three in a bed, sixteen to a table
eighty in the room of looms
> *times with no one near*
> *smell of hay*

lint and whale oil fumes from lamps
windows nailed shut
> *a brook, an arbor of wild grapes,*
> *a cool spring near the rocks*

lectures, courses, famous speakers
lots of sweets, plumcakes
> *not as fresh as in the country*

only a few minutes at table
  *no hurry when we eat*

work tries the patience
  *to be at home*
  *please, if you would*

send a few pots of plants and flowers
to the mill     for us

# Regulations
*Lawrence Manufacturing Company, 1833*

No one may be dishonest, dissolute, indolent.
All must refrain from ardent spirit, gambling, any desire
to smoke Egyptian cigarettes. Fire we must prevent.

From public worship, no one may be absent.
All must obey Sabbath rules, this we require.
No one may be dishonest, dissolute, indolent.

For advice, those far from parents may apply to the Agent.
To the utmost efficiency all must aspire
and avoid using clay pipes. Calamity we must prevent.

Encouraging moral conduct is the company's intent.
Frivolous conversation is not allowed or admired.
No one may be dishonest, dissolute, indolent.

Each worker will live in a boarding house as tenant.
We offer a year's contract for those we acquire.
No smoking in the boarding house. Flames we must prevent.

To serve here what is asked is voluntary consent.
We cherish respect, conciliation between us and all hires.
No one may be dishonest, dissolute, indolent
or linger smoking anywhere. We must prevent fires.

## CLAY PIPE

Your cup, nearly bone
white, a silent cheek
for the sweet tobacco.

I suck your shank
inhaling relief
holding on for dear life

away from that floor
that vibrates beneath my feet
in the room of iron pounding

where I sweat as burning
whale oil clogs my throat.
I keep on lifting.

Behind the boarding house
they don't care as long
as they can't see us.

We gather and pass you
one to the other, snip your stem,
each of us receives your pleasure.

Sometimes after the last bell
I go outside and light you,
watch your smoke swirl

up the brick wall past windows,
as though drawing
inside heat to open air.

I see the moon sprinkle
gold on the mill stream
and dream a life away from here.

## TURN-OUT, 1834

From the upper rooms
women walk out.
In the lower rooms
those who discussed strike hesitate.

*Should we?* then Harriet's
*I don't care. I'm turning out.*
This girl of eleven leads a line
into the street where others stream

from brick mills so much water
bursting the dam
suddenly weak
with the weight of heavy looms

and arms lifting.
Young women aging fast
from movements repeated.
Their lines become a river

moving down Amory Street—
all energy, purpose—a fullness
forgets the sore body
in the joy of marching,

remembers how they'd believed
they were in this
with the owners
until the wave struck:

> *give up wages take a cut but*
> *keep on producing as much*
> *live with five roommates*
> *instead of three*

The overseer fired the girl
who urged them to quit,
make a run on the banks.
As she left the office

she waved her bonnet in the air,
a signal to all
watching from the windows—
follow me

and they did. They rallied, they resolved:

> *we will not go back*
> *unless our wages continue*

> *we will not go back*
> *unless they receive us all as one*

> *we will not go back*

Daughters of free men
left their places
turning out a line in history—
its length: eight hundred women.

## FIGHT FOR THE TEN HOUR DAY

*based on petitions*
*to the Honorable Senate and House of Representatives*
*in General Court assembled,*
*Commonwealth of Massachusetts, 1845*

You have in hand three signed petitions
from over two thousand. In our dismay,
mostly women, we write of contagion, privation
toiling fourteen hours a day,

breathing poison air by the looms, we stay
inside barred from proper physical exercise
and send home what's needed, much of our pay.
Exhausted. How can any mind realize

its vigor?  Now as we organize
you will learn the perils of our labor.
Joined together we recognize
your power to make change in our favor:

*let no body employ one set of hands*
*more than ten hours a day—this, our urgent demand.*

## THE COMMITTEE RESPONDS
*based on Massachusetts House Document no. 50*

We gathered many facts in relation to
the Hours of Labor. The average each day
in the Lowell mills—twelve and a half.

> Sarah Bagley works by the piece.
> *Chief evil: shortness of time for meals.*
> *Next evil: no time to cultivate the mind.*

Dr. Wells, city physician found less sickness
here than elsewhere, fewer dying
in Lowell this year than last.

> Petitioners respond. *Females taken sick in Lowell*
> *return home and die. One girl fell down, broke*
> *her neck which led to instant death.*

Mr. Isaac Cooper Member of the House, overseer
at a mill, said girls enjoy the best health.
Early to bed, early to rise, three meals regular.

> Olive Clark favors the ten-hour system.
> *The long hours affected my health, my breath.*
> *Small balls of cotton fly about.*

We visited and saw grass plats laid out
and within, cultivated flowers
all aimed at health and comfort.

> Mr. Abbot at the Lawrence Corporation
> was asked to appear. His boss instructed,
> *Go, but say as little as possible.*

Restricting the hours, we could not compete.
Better if they were less, the air pure, more time to eat,
but the remedy is not with us.

> Sarah Bagley complained. *Whatever*
> *was given was made to say*
> *what we never said or thought of saying.*

In conclusion, the remedy lies in more love
for social happiness, a higher appreciation
for man's destiny, in less love for money.

> *They shaped the whole to please the aristocrats.*
> *In the next one we'll ask them to extend us*
> *the same protection they give animals.*

## NIGHT WRITERS

because they wrote     we
know   so many at table     only
twenty minutes between bells

    *food in large bowls*
    *a frantic kind of eating*

wanting to leave space     in their mouths
for words     but the hunger     oh
they'd earned this meat     standing
since dawn by the looms

    *breath clogged     the heat*
    *of lint     moist air*

they wanted     their lungs to
clear     my breath     catches
when someone     lights a wood fire
they inhaled     the foul smell
whale oil lamps     burning
through winter     the windows shut

    *we all need breath*
    *to make words*

what I'm telling     they wrote
grabbed from the weaving     from Bibles
they hid     from the one who
didn't survive     her long hair
scalped by the machine     at night
with stiff hands     hacking croup
stubborn to write     they held pens

## Two Cent Bridge

Makers of paper
crossed on their way

home to factory
then home again.

A scripted offering
in each extended hand

two pennies each
for the toll booth man.

Dark in the morning,
dark at night.

They waited all year for light.
Her two feet, his aching arms

across that bridge we stroll
time on our hands,

above the still racing Kennebec
one falls to the next,

near the man asleep in the sun
flushed cheeks, mouth undone,

near the tavern
of drunk fights and arrests,

and maybe you did
your own hard drinking then.

From one side to the other
morning entered night,

home became factory,
dark extinguished light.

## To Cleanse

Across the street she sweeps
holding the pale handle. My muscles

recognize this motion that repeats,
learned in girlhood. The eye

catches clouds of dog hair
or the pavement's sand, conveys

its message to the limbic brain
which sends us to find the broom

then discard what we cannot
erase or shove underneath.

The street sweepers come
to clear debris.

Somewhere the ocean's waves
advance and retreat brushing the sand.

This rustle I hear in the trees
is the rise and fall of sparrow wings.

## HOME

We were nomads in those years,
inhabiting other people's houses
when they were gone, wanting
to curl into the safety of what they'd left,
wanting our faith restored in rooms so neatly
arranged, kitchens full of every kind of utensil,
back gardens where peas lined up
and beans were ready to break.

But shadows slid under doors,
and a slippery sheen of grey held.
We were caught between dense trees at dusk
the wind jostled and a road
emptying over and over;
and cast out from where the grapevine
framed an entrance, as sunlight traced itself
in eagerness along the walls.

Edging ahead, it took years to uncover:
the soul is the only home the body ever knows.

## Applause

a rich sound, like turbines
when water rushes through them

surge of energy
erupting but sustained

outpouring of excitement
arriving in the hands

shared ocean of Hosannas
release from the self's cave

an offering to those
who stand before us

when their gifts
have been received

# III

# ARK

## The River's Frozen Bank

Tracks along the white path
reach the bank
then disappear in ice—
the frozen river's woody glass
holds slowed life.

I stick to the shore—
far from the house.
At my feet
prints crowd the snow
where deer bent to eat.

The dry reeds' tassels
speak in rasping whispers,
but spring and I know
they will spread
a ruddy endurance.

I bend, rest my arms
on the crabapple's overhanging limb
as wind rocks us both—
moving through me,
then beyond.

## RIVER TRACKS

Who but Jesus walks on water?
And I'm not sure about him. Footprints
must end where the river begins.
But I see them anyway—huge pockets
tracking from one shore to the other
before water fills in.

Near the bank, a dream-laden train
always leaps, clacking through a childhood
home to reclaim a death the parents—
in their own notion of protecting—had hidden.

And the avalanche repeats—Hitler's rock face
on the Palisades breaking apart with a terrible
rumbling. The grownups like frightened children,
race the trolley non-stop, believing
the war has finally brought home bombs.

I need to walk on sand,
but water extends. I remember those before,
all claimed by the trains and the river
into a living sleep. Their tracks
form, dissolve, form again.

## BACKYARD DIG

Digging I found toys in my garden,
plastic figures two inches high:

a pale businessman in suit, hat, tie,
briefcase in his right hand.

He comes from my father's time,
lone commuter about to step down.

Then this bright red fireman, eyes
hidden behind an oxygen mask, ax in his hand.

Difficult to locate his decade
though he's headed for a serious fire

and maybe remembers
his gas mask from the war.

None dances with a partner.
Not one is poised to turn a book's pages.

There are others, too—
cowboys, a Greek soldier—

each carrying what his world demanded,
each right hand directed.

Now I see how they are burdened
—briefcase, ax,

the gun I envied
and never named.

## SUNSET AT PIER 60

Wrapped in fastened belts and padlocked chains
he had to get out. His father held the microphone
blaring out the seconds. Promised
his son would beat Houdini's record.
We surrounded in a thick circle

our eyes fixed, wanting this son
to break out, but not too easily. We wanted
the struggle, the nearly-not-making it
moments before the final release.

Slender in the extreme, no longer boy, he swung
his enchained upper body furiously, dipped so close
to earth we feared his head would split on packed
earth, swung in a circle, righted himself,
drew a gasping breath, swung again. That sigh

from us when the chains catapulted
like a waterfall over his head. More wriggling
to make his way out of the locked vest, almost
too fast as the whole thing clattered down.
He stepped away from the pile of metal.

Excited, relieved, I wished
the son could leap far away
from this grim narrative that held me fast.

His father passed the hat.

# WEIRD

Of course the circus sideshow
with the by-now-familiar sword-eating fellow,
the Siamese twins, maybe a bearded lady,
sticky pink cotton candy
down in Madison Square Garden
where nothing grows, but something
would grow in my dream of jumping beans.
Arranged in certain patterns
they began leaping together
as though they enjoyed being planted
with each other. In the you-tube clip
the twenty-somethings pop corn
with cell phones. Once the ring tones sing,
*voila*, wow, corn flies like fourth of July
fireworks that are kind of ecstatic with color,
noise, that red-white-blue freedom fervor,
freedom to pop corn and blow things up,
the way bombs dropped from high places,
go off in the middle of someone's street,
or the kitchen,
and the part that's incredibly weird is
being taught     *thou shalt not kill*
then later     *how to kill*
and also     *come home and don't kill now,*
and if you do   it's called murder,
and     *we'll kill you*     for that.
Oh, you will have a religious guide
to sit with you before you are marched
down the hard corridor. That's when
you need a bomb to fall and make
a hole in the wall so you can run
through the circle. When the lights
flickered in Yonkers they said,
"Someone's getting zapped in Sing Sing."

## It Says

new   young
it says   very bright
beauty and logo
brand   wear it
let it show
be labeled
new   young

it says dark   shiny
newly polished
upholstery smell
still fresh
outgassing
plastic

it says Sears
Walmart
Disney

it says
sewing machines
lined up   dead
gray with ash
factory floor
fading shades
like dirty snow

it says
locked in
it says
smoke   bodies
gray stretchers
carried out

it says
shop
buy bargains
guaranteed

it says
so cheap

## YOLKS

Forsythia's here with its bold assertion,
a yellow like the yolks of Americana eggs
we had for breakfast delivered from his farm
where money's the problem—a wife's sister,
horses and chickens to feed, then a rat
slipping in at night to eat the eggs. He

was careful to place poison deep in the wall.
The dead rat was larger and furrier
than expected, velvety brown, a rat inviting
touch. He seemed to love the rat,
giving him credit for uniqueness.
He didn't take a photograph.

We can love what we destroy. Or is it
the other way around? How the passions
collide, although I wouldn't
call his impulse hate, more irritation, more
needing those eggs, needing to keep
the feeding and gathering rituals intact.

Killing has a host of reasons. We even joked
about murdering the obese sister who drains
the farm's kitty with her hip surgeries, her horses.
Never pays, she's had it this way thirty
years, a place to pretend she's somebody
of the horsey set. Takes what the family has

too little of, arms outstretched. Will go on
taking like the rat who had to be stopped.

# Ice Storm

*Suddenly I came to dwell inside*
*this confusion of shatterings.*

I had to roll the windows down,
break the icy panes.
They fell outside and inside hardly melting.

*How delicate sounds convey what*
*wants to remain forgotten, verboten.*

Sound of shattering. November long
past, the shop windows smashed.
Why a rain of falling glass now on Ash Wednesday?

*Thrown glass smashing. Are the figures bent*
*toward one another embracing or about to push away?*

"If it's necessary, please, hide my child."
One mother, then another, plead
hearing the crystal sound.

*Under the weight of ice, secrets, ice age memories,*
*carried back into cells that hold them.*

How thin the borders between ice and glass.
Ice and glass break thin skin.
I need to see each lost face again.

*Clarity of ice encasing branches.*
*Clarity of sun hitting ice, enough thaw*

On the incline, someone
offered me a hand. I held it, then gave mine.
We made a chain of three, sliding.

> *to hear a crack, splatter of broken egg,*
> *demon crack in the ice in the egg*

Later, strangers ventured fearfully
beneath a listless horizon.

> *the awful splatter and breaking, spilling*
> *of life on the pavement. Out of the cherished crock.*

## SAM'S ADVICE

Someone who's lost
needs a useful thing to do
like chopping
and hauling. Even slopping

feed to the hogs
you can take pride in that,
but you may have a wife
not showing respect. Mine didn't.

It's quite possible
I hit her then—
I sure wanted to—losing her
into the piney night.

These days I feel good
when Perry and I bury fence posts
and gather wood on his farm
where the sun's up early

and days go
at the speed they should—
you work, get tired and sleep
in your own bed at night

not minding dreams
or silver needles
sliding like women
away from the trees.

## Next Day

One day followed the next until
    suddenly evening.

Rain bent branches;
    drops slid from their tips and fell.

Soothsayers' forked beards
    tangled in the marshes.

Where there had been many kinds,
    graveyards held animals we'd counted.

We were mired between dire predictions
    and our predilections.

The animals had been named—
    there were efforts—but no one appointed.

Somehow a collective dream was forming,
    its mist offering frail handles.

The dog knew to tuck paws under head,
    her body a whorl, then she slept.

# ARK

Asleep in the ark of bed,
the wife, the husband, the dog
wrapped in bunched bedclothes
each with a special way
of breathing. Sometimes breath
signals from the dream—
a quickening of garbled words,
a sigh. Sometimes dreams
escape in the dark room.

Dead parents appear young,
able to talk and walk.
The dog whimpers remembering
her early confinement.
A friend returns with a message:
*all you need lies within.*

Bedded down, the pack rests.
The edges yield as the ark
rocks, retrieving the ones lost.
Beyond the room's windows,
a deep breath of stars
enters night's ocean.

## WILD RIVER

It is a quiet I borrow from the leaves
as they fall toward the center.
Oh let light continue to play
where one misty morning,
the mockingbird rushed into flight
revealing white patches on its wings.

Have I grown too far into solitude,
this conversation with myself?
I remember taking a photograph
facing the mirror, at maybe twelve
or thirteen, the pink diary I would burn later
closed on the dresser's top.

Still I recognize the long-haired girl
whose gaze was there and not there,
working to stay in the middle,
then leaving quickly as the bird
must be doing whose song a minute ago
was vivid, but now grows faint.

Fighting to stay,
and afraid of the quiet's
seduction, that I shall enter a place
of only leaves, birds, dreams.

Once I rode as a passenger on a wild river.
Our guide was distracted briefly
at a critical moment,
pulled the raft in far and late,
nearly missed the scouting point,
last stop before the final treacherous run.

Trying to stay at the center and moving quickly,
I made an almost fatal mistake. I've never learned
how to travel the river safely,
never believed I could be safe,
and it's not the river I fear,
but the people who navigate.

## GREEN HERON

*Praises be*
*grateful me*
*a silver canoe*
*you*
*and the green heron*


Your eye keened on the green
heron traipsing the bank,
us adrift in water lilies
I'd bent to touch, my fingers
trailing the rippled surface.

From stern to bow, between us
a line of whispers—your sightings—
something the wide sky
and the lake water understood
as if you belonged to them.

The bird on delicate legs was
in and out of shrubs at the edge
until drawn by the rustle of prey
his neck and beak extended, he suddenly flew—
a line of energy tied to a bowl of feathers.

## WALKING WORLD

Leave me here
where sun splashes frozen snow
and ice ridges press underfoot,

where yesterday
I glimpsed a coyote
loping near the wall.

He might have been rabid,
venturing out mid-day.
Or very hungry.

His was a body caught by the season
moving along at a steady gait,
seeming indifferent to the world beyond his path.

Looking back I wonder,
did he eat before his long day ended?
Was she on her way to feed babies in the den?

What does any creature do?

     —that lean body moving,
     then gone.

## Forest Trail

We were watching the bull
whose hoof pawed air,
and none of us rushed in
despite the steps
four up, four down
into the pasture.
We retreated to the bed of tracks
stretched like a fallen ladder.

But this was the chosen trail,
and we meant to travel its length,
circling beyond the bull's sight
to slip under barbed wire,
our way into the forest

where light made slats
on the wide path
through the pine's dark cover
and gold-leafed maples
bobbed in the late fall air
like saints' heads in halos.
Our laughter climbed high
as bittersweet on the branches.

## Marion Cemetery

In the promised shade beneath
ancient sugar maples,
summer shadows climb the shallow
hills, cool the gravelly road.

The sign says *no pets allowed*,
and you are anxious to avoid
an upbraiding from some lurking
guard. *Let's leave*, you urge.

I want to allow the breeze,
want the dog to sniff
each delicate blade
surrounding rows of markers

for the misbegotten and the cherished.
Gabriel stands over them, his
wings stretched to his ankles
near a plain stone that says simply *wife*.

Death's not chasing me
here—the dates, the names all present,
lives already spent, this stone
crafted into a broken trunk.

A white van approaches. *They've
come for us*, but no,
dear one, not this time.
The driver merely smiles and waves.

## On Peter's Hill

Because we can both walk,
and you are at my side or somewhere
behind taking the pictures
I try to capture in words
of this landscape we inhale,
let me say how

in the light of a cantaloupe sunset
that skyscraper on the horizon
is a gleaming tower of gold.
And how, to our left,
those shadowed pines are adorned
by a lace of weeping cherries.

Remember, whatever comes next,
we have walked here.

# EPILOGUE

## SUMMER, MARSHFIELD

His garden of clumped colors in beds
spread toward a wilderness
that traveled back,
touching his hair, the day–
old beard, his sheaf of skin.

Chickadees signaled their pecking order,
and, through the high grass, human
voices marked the nearness of neighbors.
Inside the fence, pale lettuce had been nibbled,
but most of his well-tended vegetables thrived,
as I did in that sun that seemed
to melt fences.

He moved with ease and, once inside,
set a bowl of raspberries on the table.
And then his willing back offered itself,
dough for my hungry fingers.

There I lived.
Sprouting moments encircled the house.
Love's sluice grew an opening in the deep canal,
and we paddled, a pilgrimage down
longing's great channel—
inside this listening      and telling
of tiny racing cells      marsh grass      rose
an ocean.

# NOTES

*Page 15:*  Phragmites are widely distributed reeds with tall stems and large panicles resembling plumes. Considered an invasive species.

*Page 19:*  Quotes from letters to J. Harold Clarke from Edgard M. Clarke written 1928-1931.

*Page 25:*  Charles Gayle is a jazz saxophonist, pianist, bass clarinetist, bassist, and percussionist.

*Page 28:*  Epigraph from *Light Years,* James Salter.

*Page 28:*  Based on information from The Stamford Historical Society and Clark, Rev. Edgar W., *The History and Genealogy of Samuel Clark, Sr. and His Descendents from 1636-1891.*

*Page 41:*  Robinson, Harriet, *Loom and Spindle,* p.38. *Cotton Mill Girls,* traditional folk song.

*Page 45:*  Larcom, Lucy, *A New England Girlhood.* Words and phrases from chapter 3, "The Hymn Book," and Chapter 7, "Beginning to Work."

*Page 47:*  Larcom, from Chapter 8, "By the River."

*Page 53:*  Based on "General Regulations to be Observed by Persons Employed by the Lawrence Manufacturing Company, in Lowell," 1833.

—Philip L. McAlary

Holly Guran, author of the chapbooks *River Tracks* (Poets Corner Press) and *Mothers' Trails* (Noctiluca Press), grew up with a view of the Hudson River which partly accounts for the frequency of rivers and water in this collection. Holly went on to live in a variety of places from Eugene, Oregon to Rome, Italy, eventually landing in Boston where she is retired from a long career at Roxbury Community College. She earned a Massachusetts Cultural Council finalist award (2012), is a member of the Jamaica Pond Poets, and has been a presenter at the Massachusetts Poetry Festival. Each summer Holly attends the Joiner Institute for the Study of War and Social Consequence where writing workshops host veterans and others. Her publications include *Salamander, Poet Lore, Poetry East, Westchester Review, U.S. Worksheets 1,* and she was a featured poet in *The Aurorean* and *Bellowing Ark*. Holly lives with her husband, Philip and their dog, Ginger, and enjoys visits with children and grandchildren.

CPSIA information can be obtained at www.ICGtesting.com
Printed in the USA
LVOW06s0738230315

431557LV00006B/8/P